Color Me Relaxed: Unique Mandala Designs For Your Relaxation

By: Lena Kez

Welcome to *Color Me Relaxed!* Mandalas are the avenue to relaxation for your stressful life. These mandalas will take you back down your childhood lane of coloring your world in creative ways. I remember many days lying on the floor with my crayons spread beside me as I chose from multiple colors to fill in the lines of my favorite coloring book.

All of these designs are original and created with your coloring quests in mind. Feel free to use colored pencils, ink pens, markers or any tool that suits your taste. Explore ways to show off contrasting colors. Place a blank page behind the mandala you're coloring to protect the pages following from color bleeds. You will find two blank pages in the back of the book for you to cut out and use for this purpose. Please feel free to photocopy as many pages as you like so you can keep your book in pristine condition. Enjoy and have fun!

Join me on Facebook for one free weekly design: https://www.facebook.com/artistlenakez

Follow me on Twitter: https://twitter.com/LenaKez

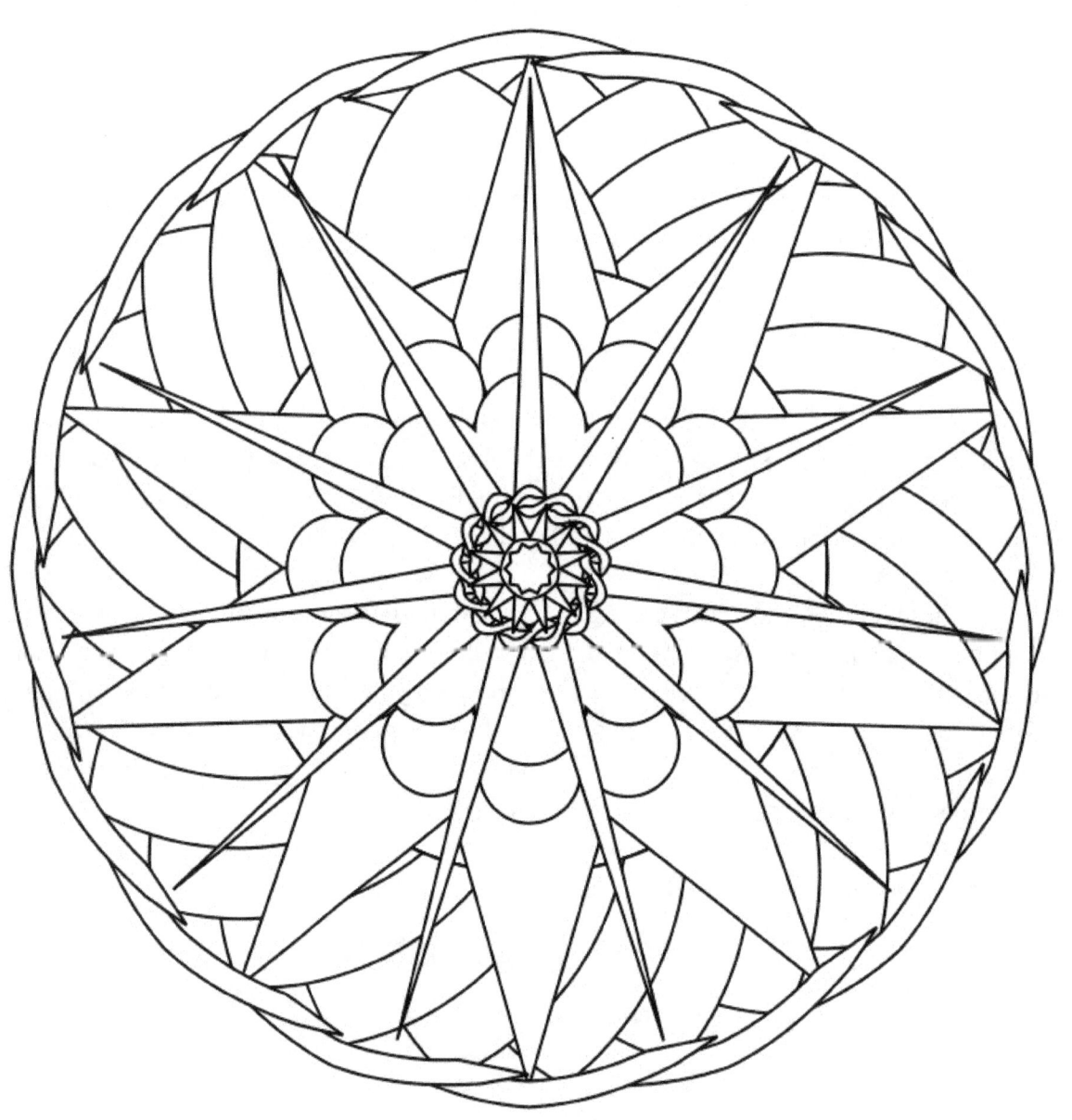

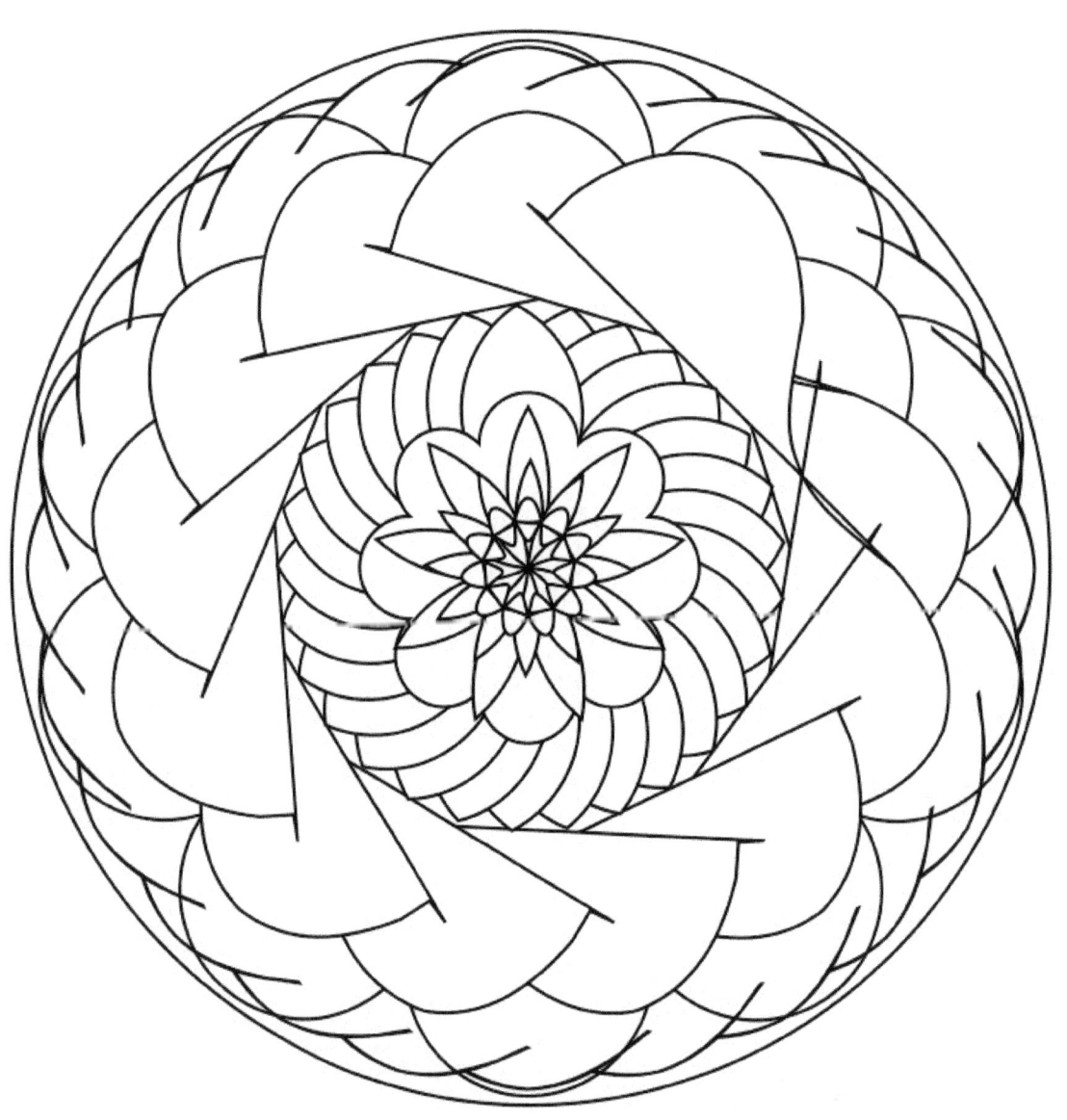

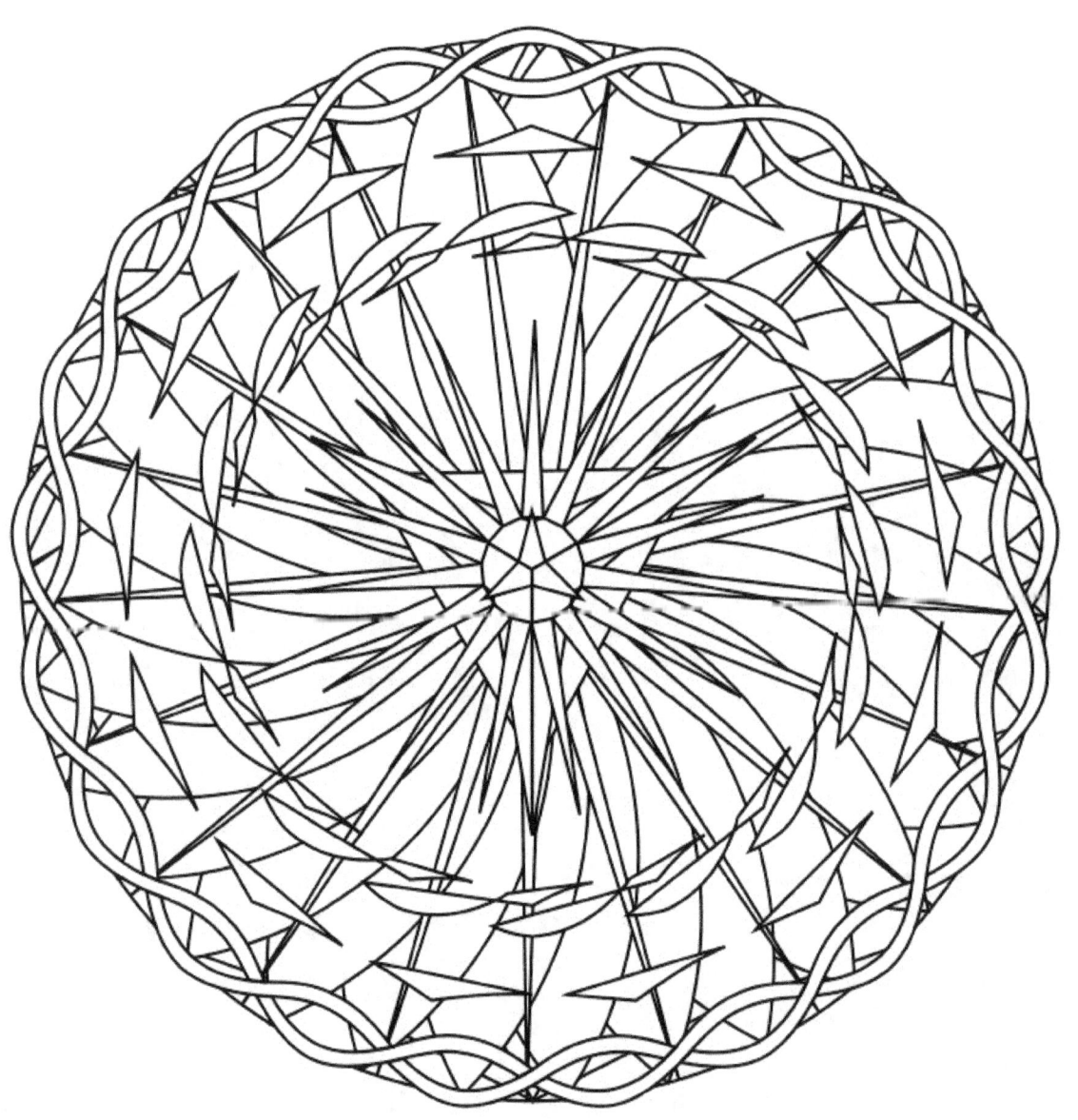

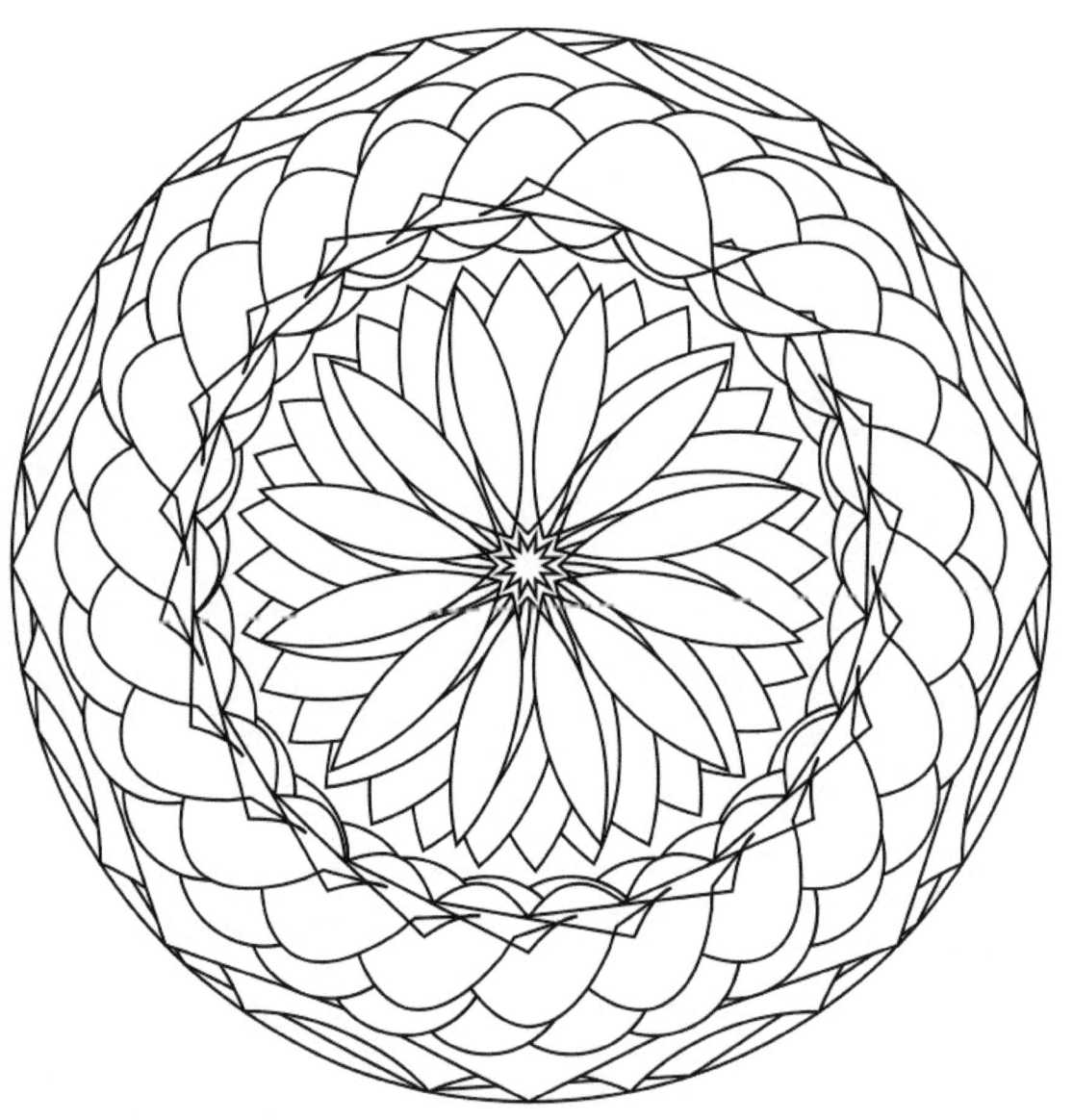

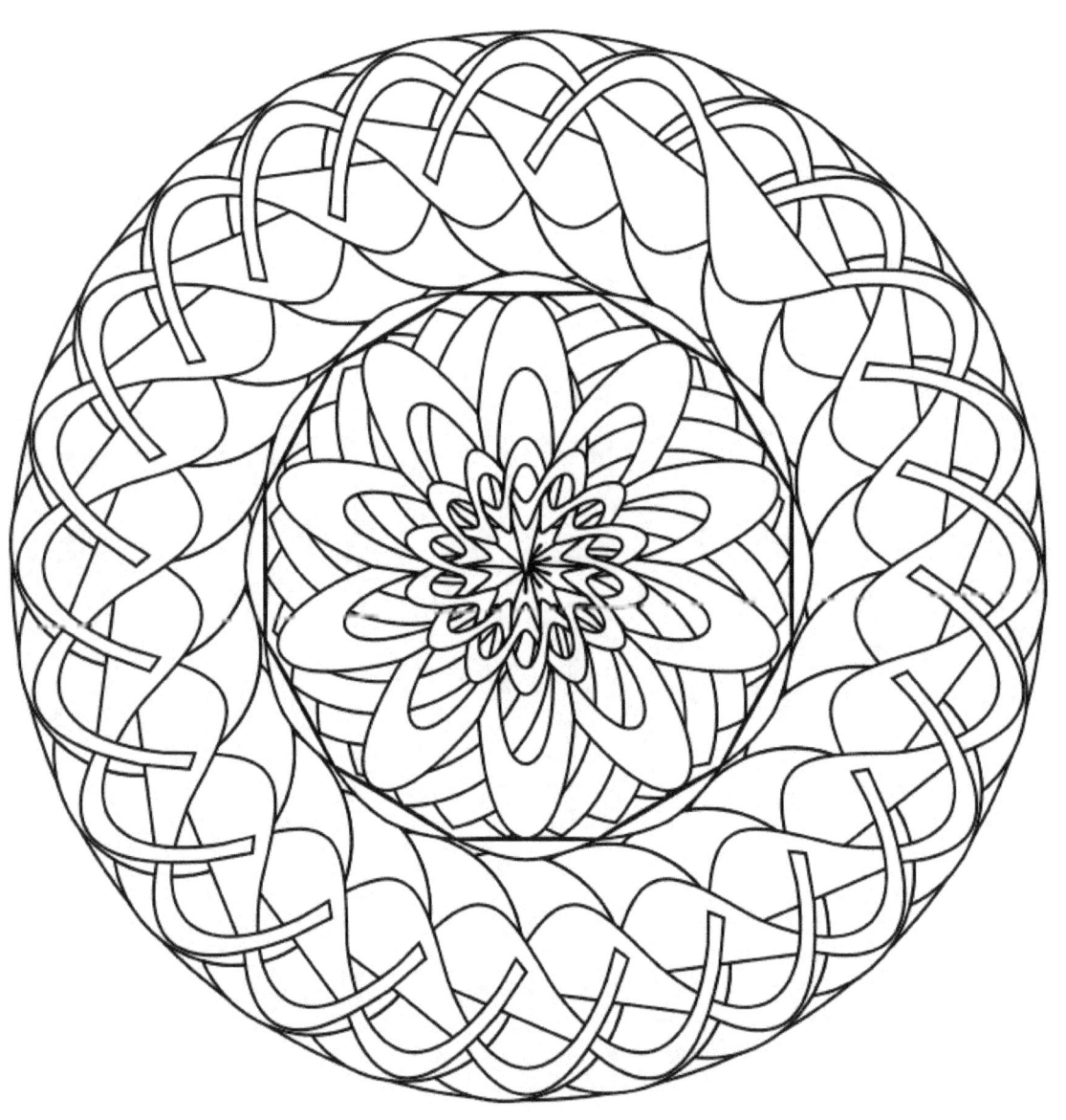

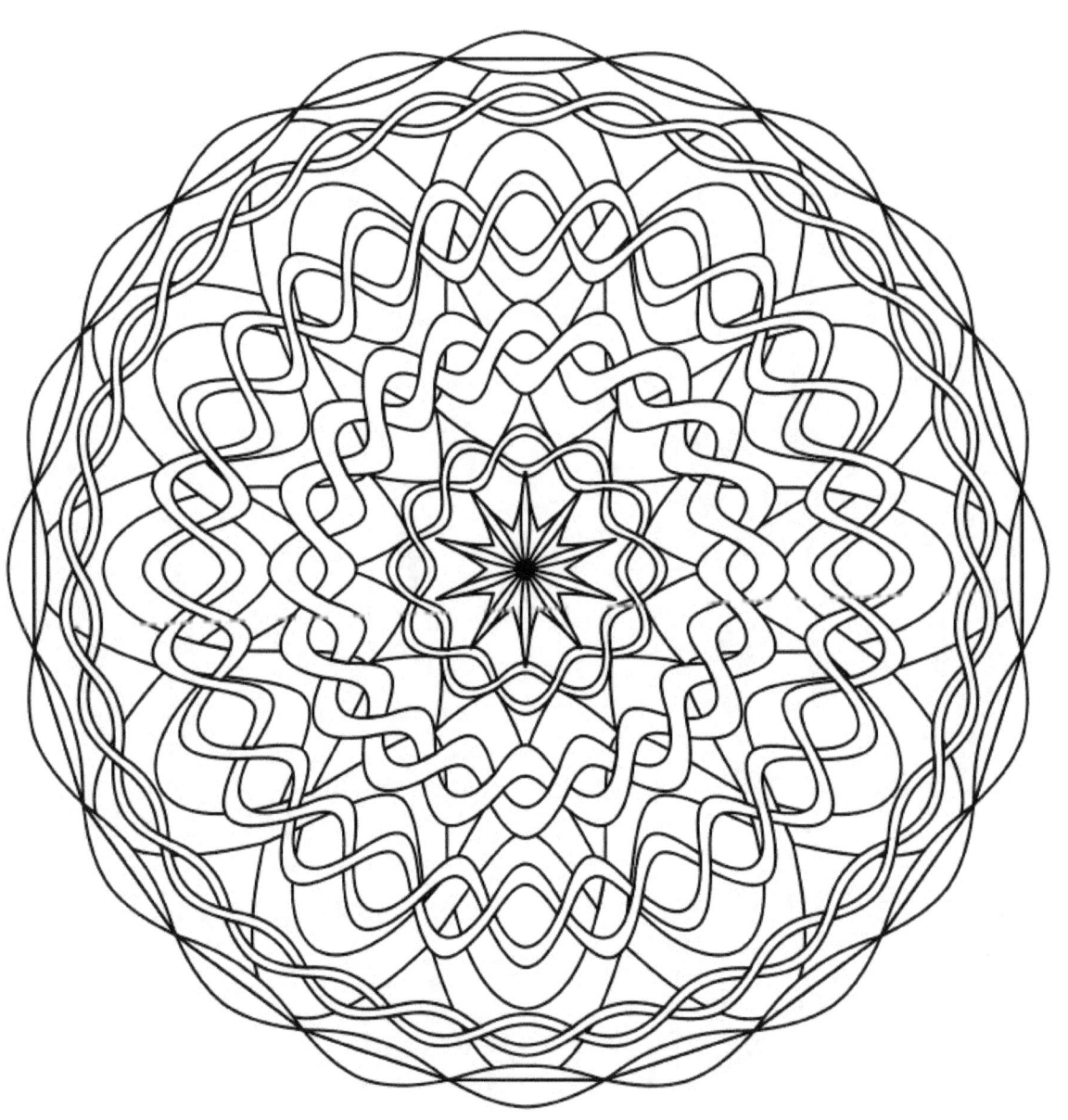

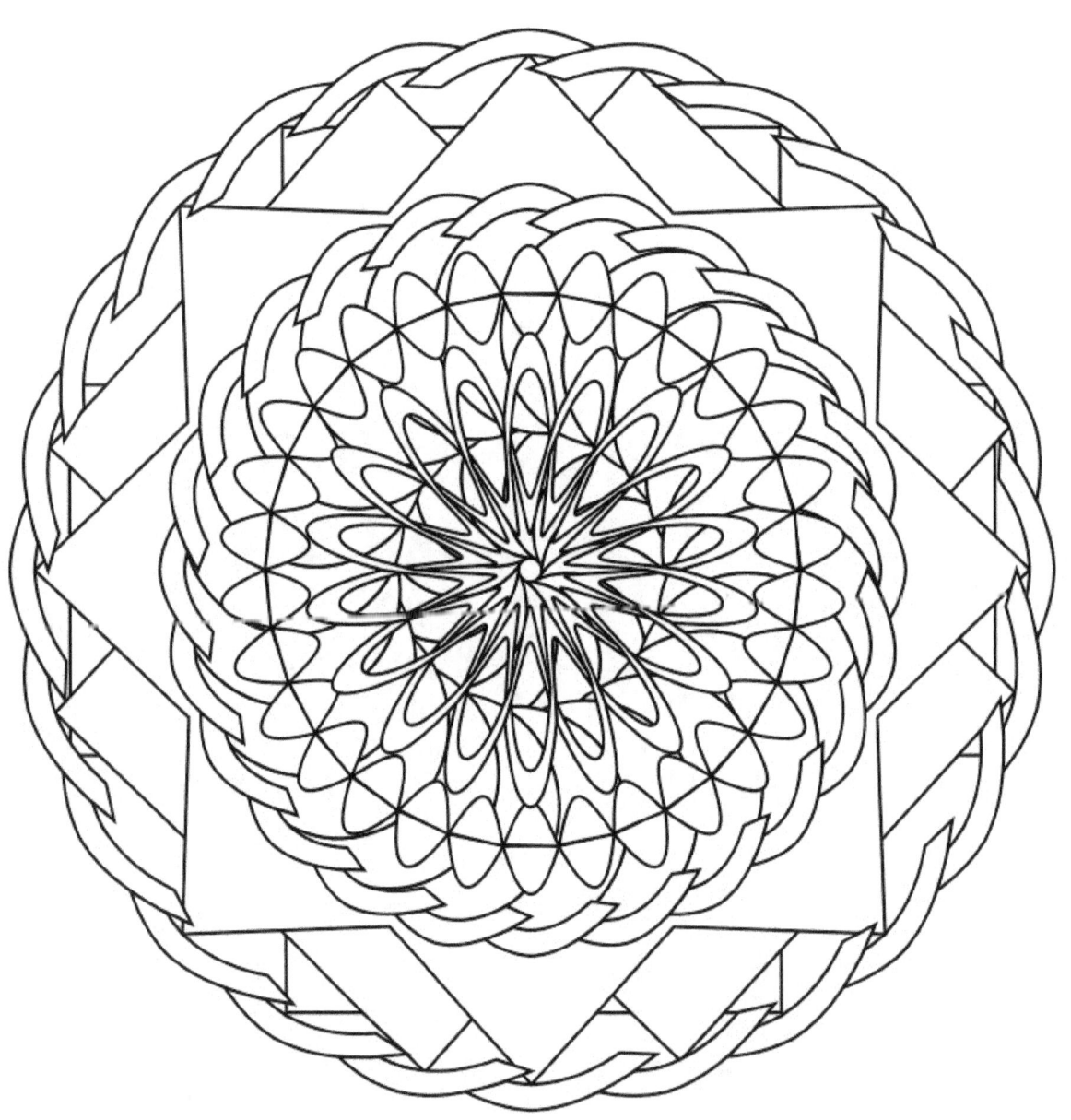

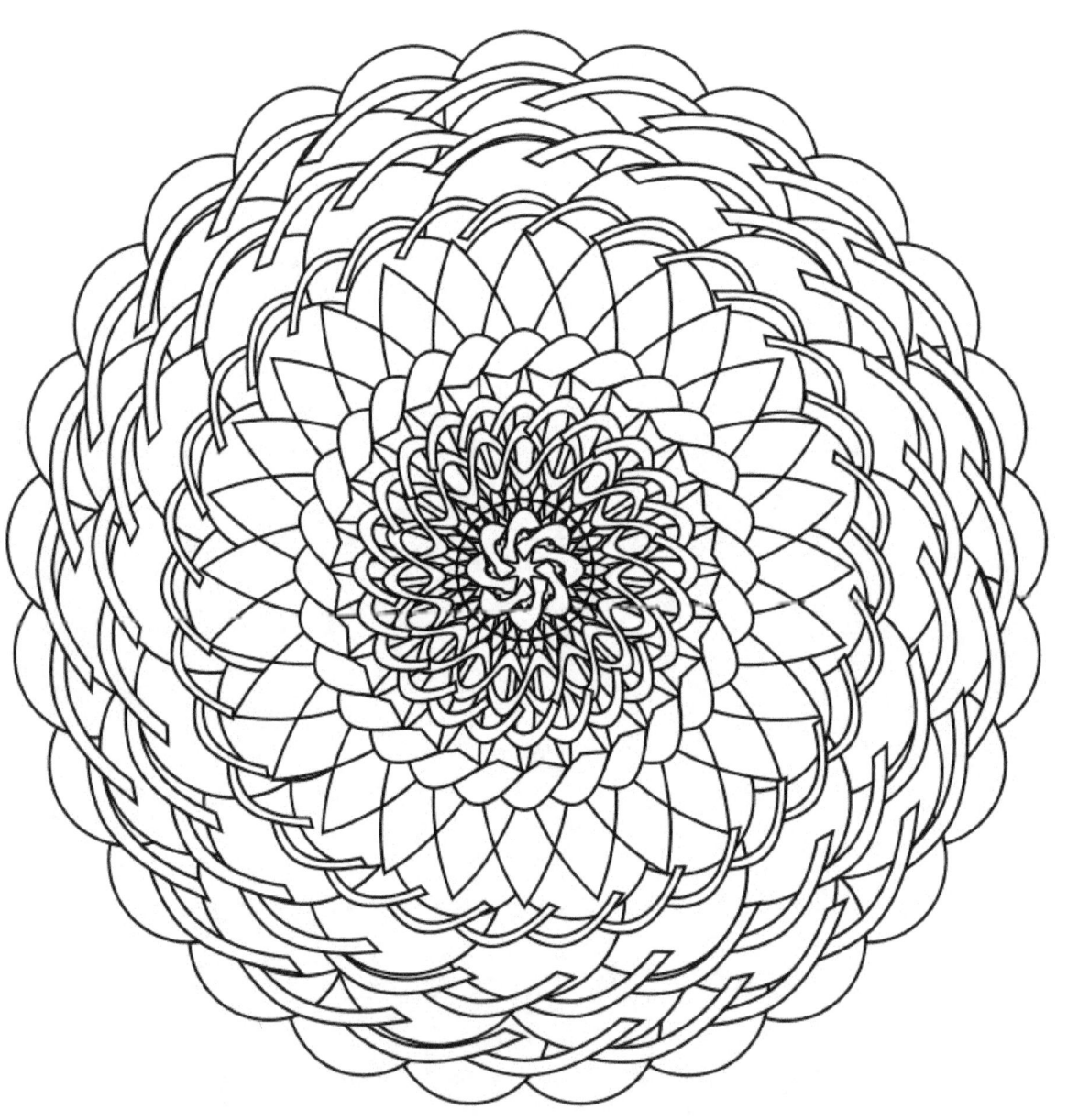

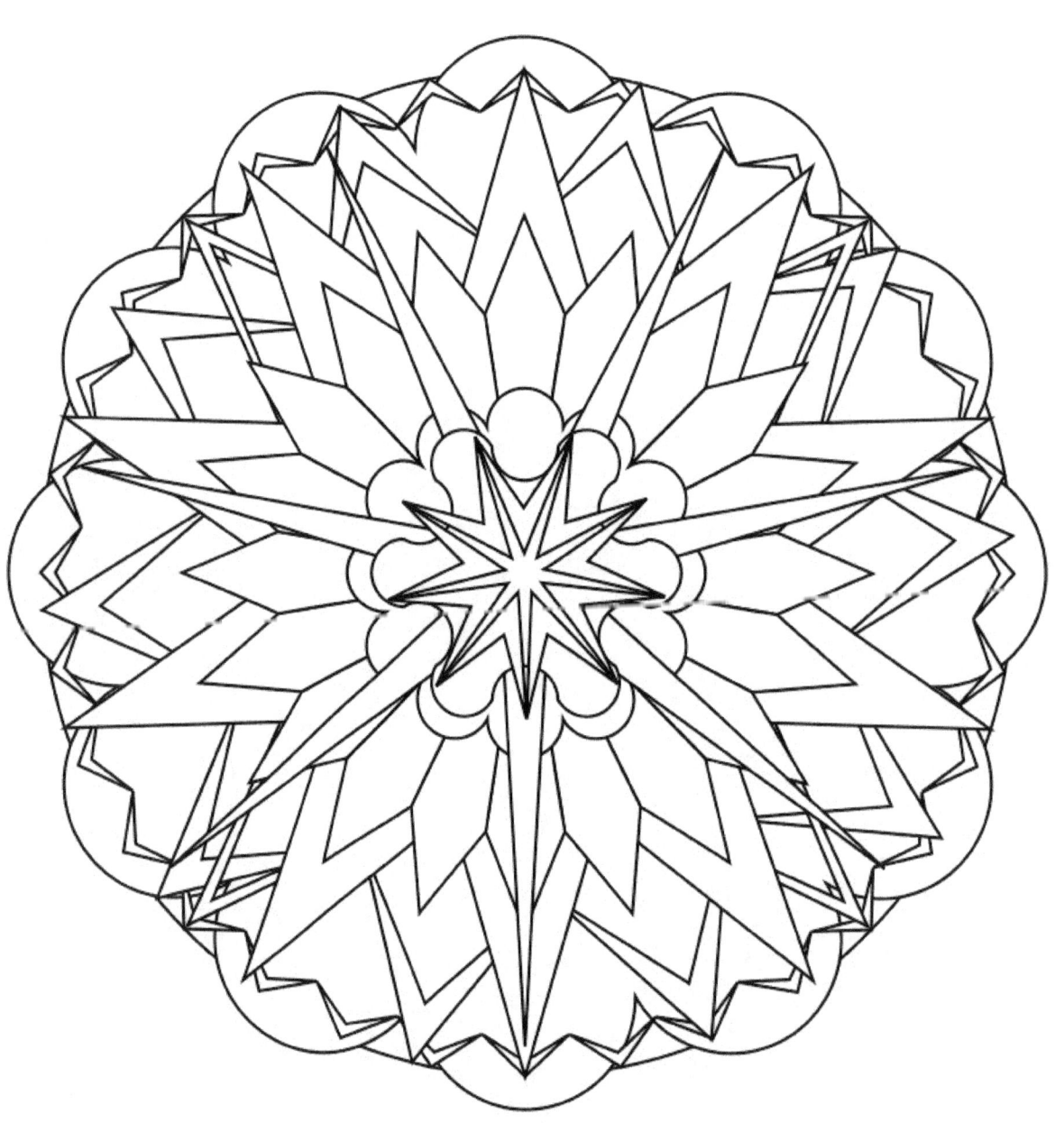

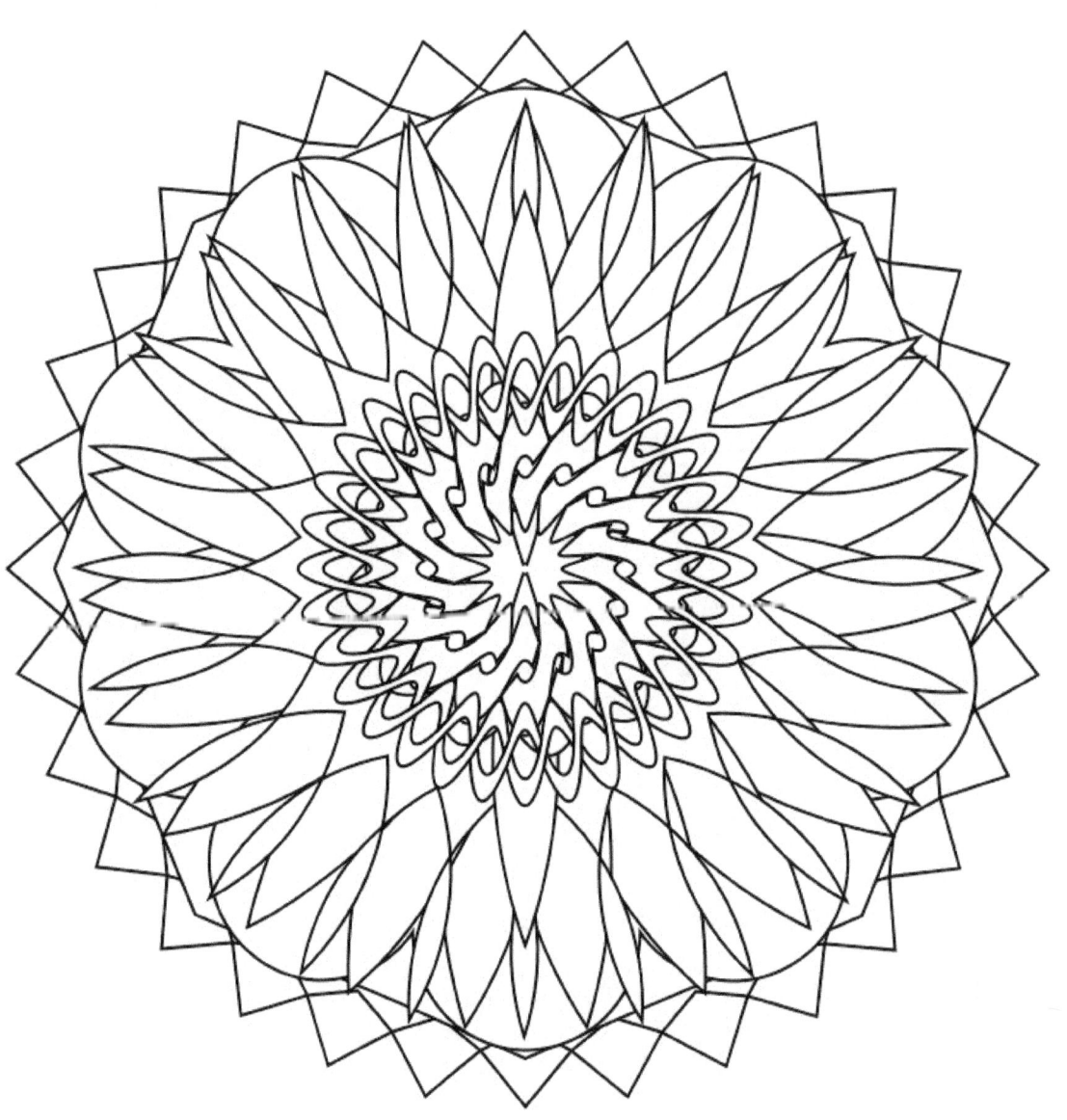

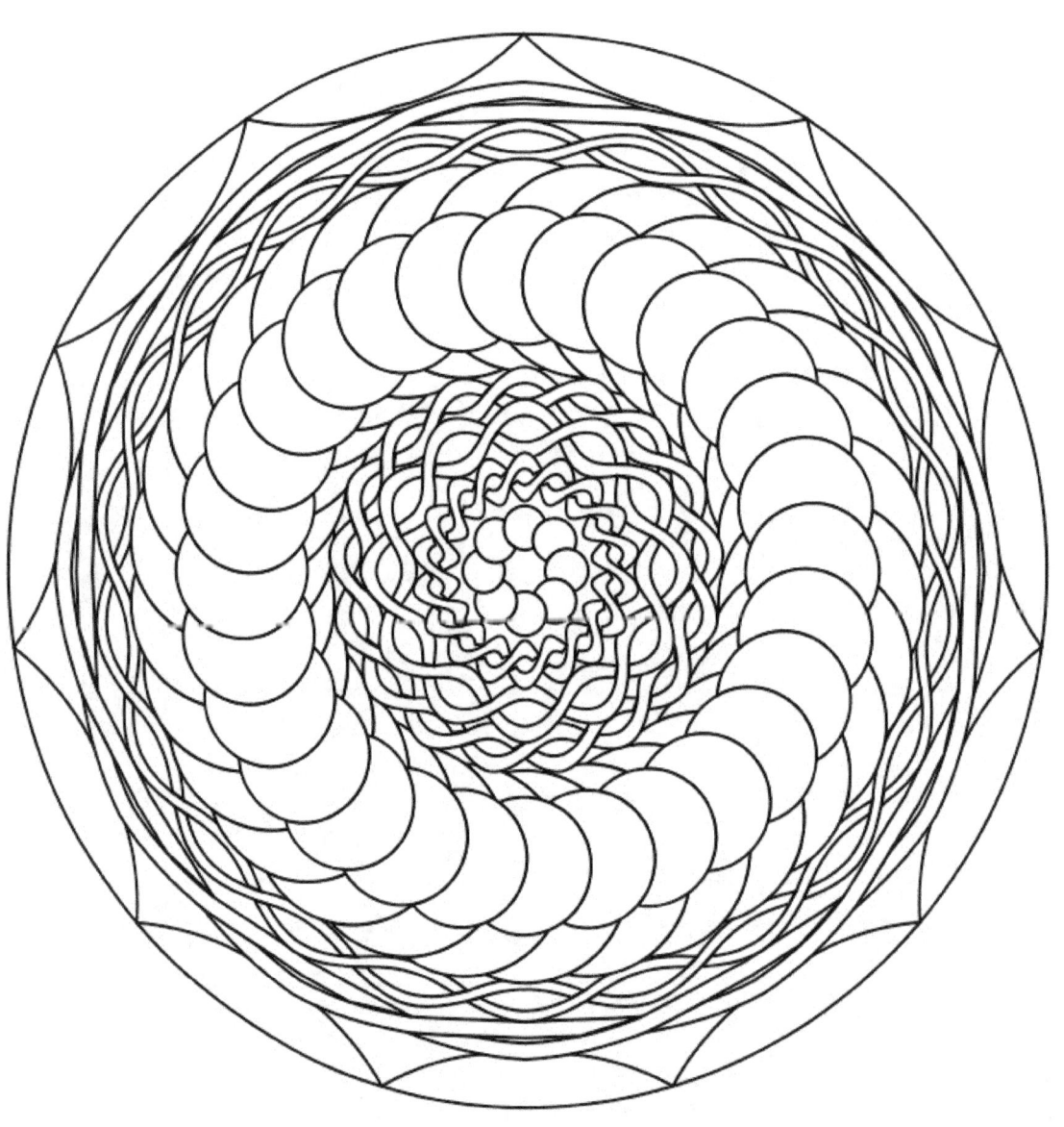

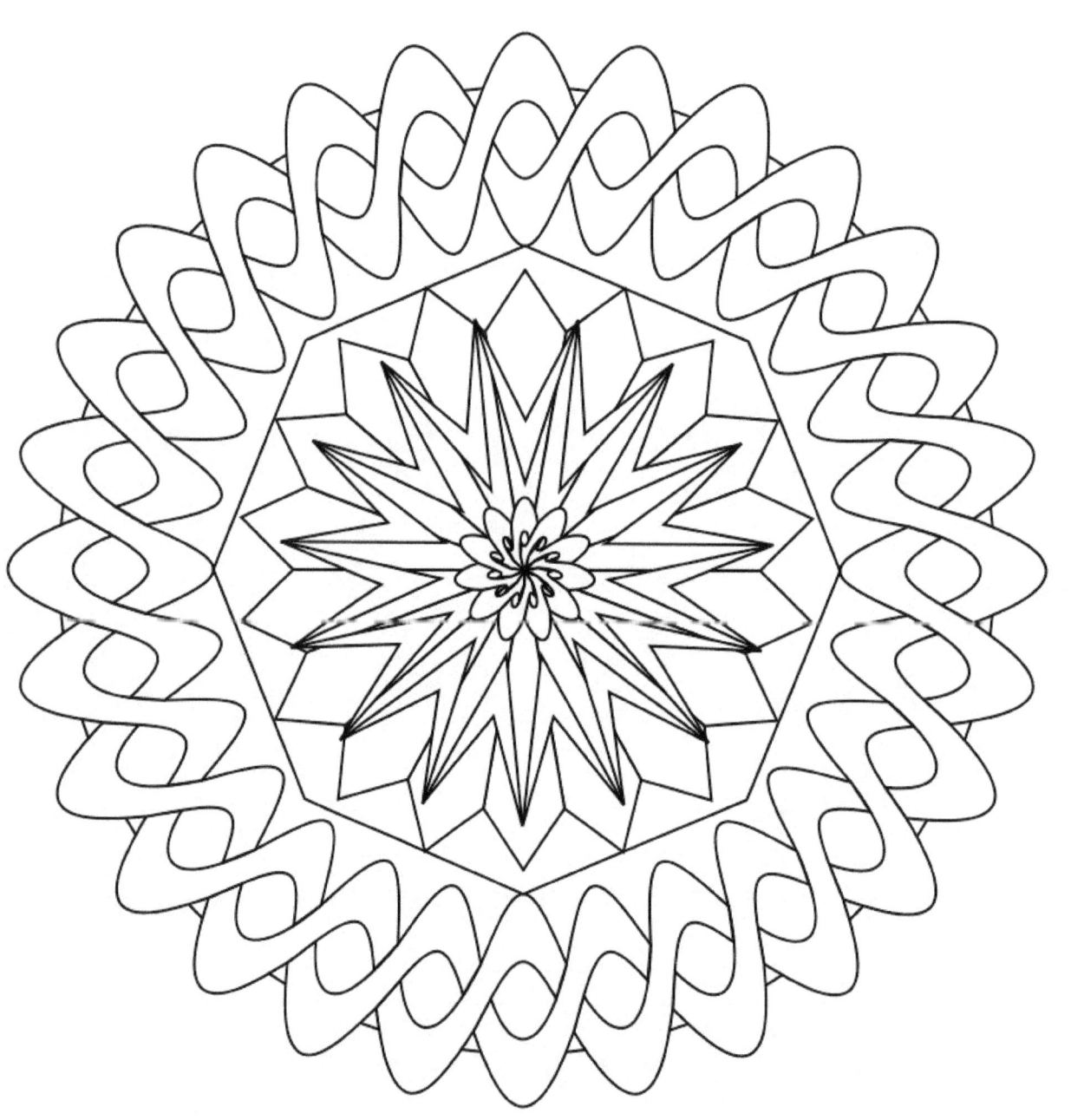

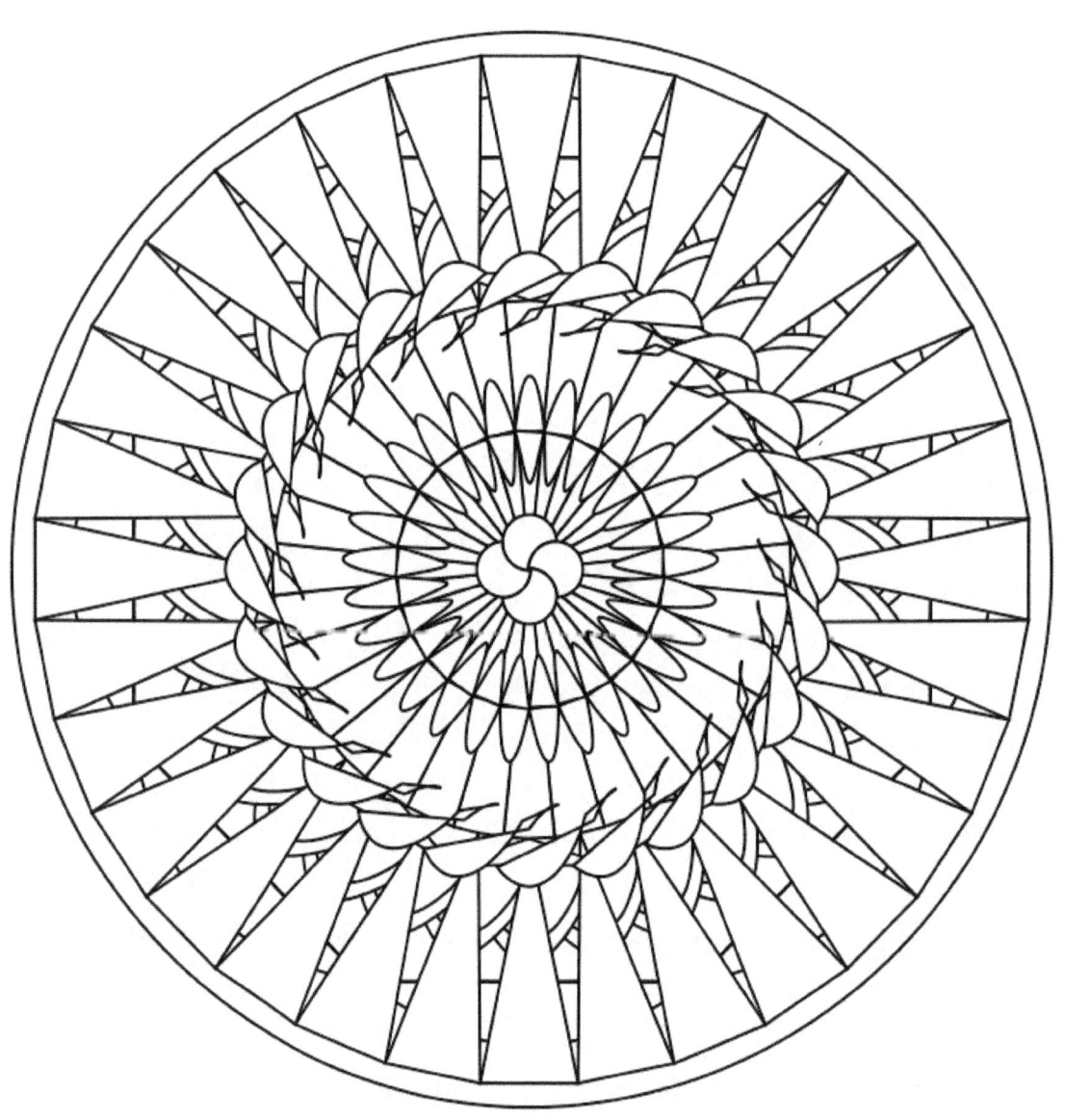

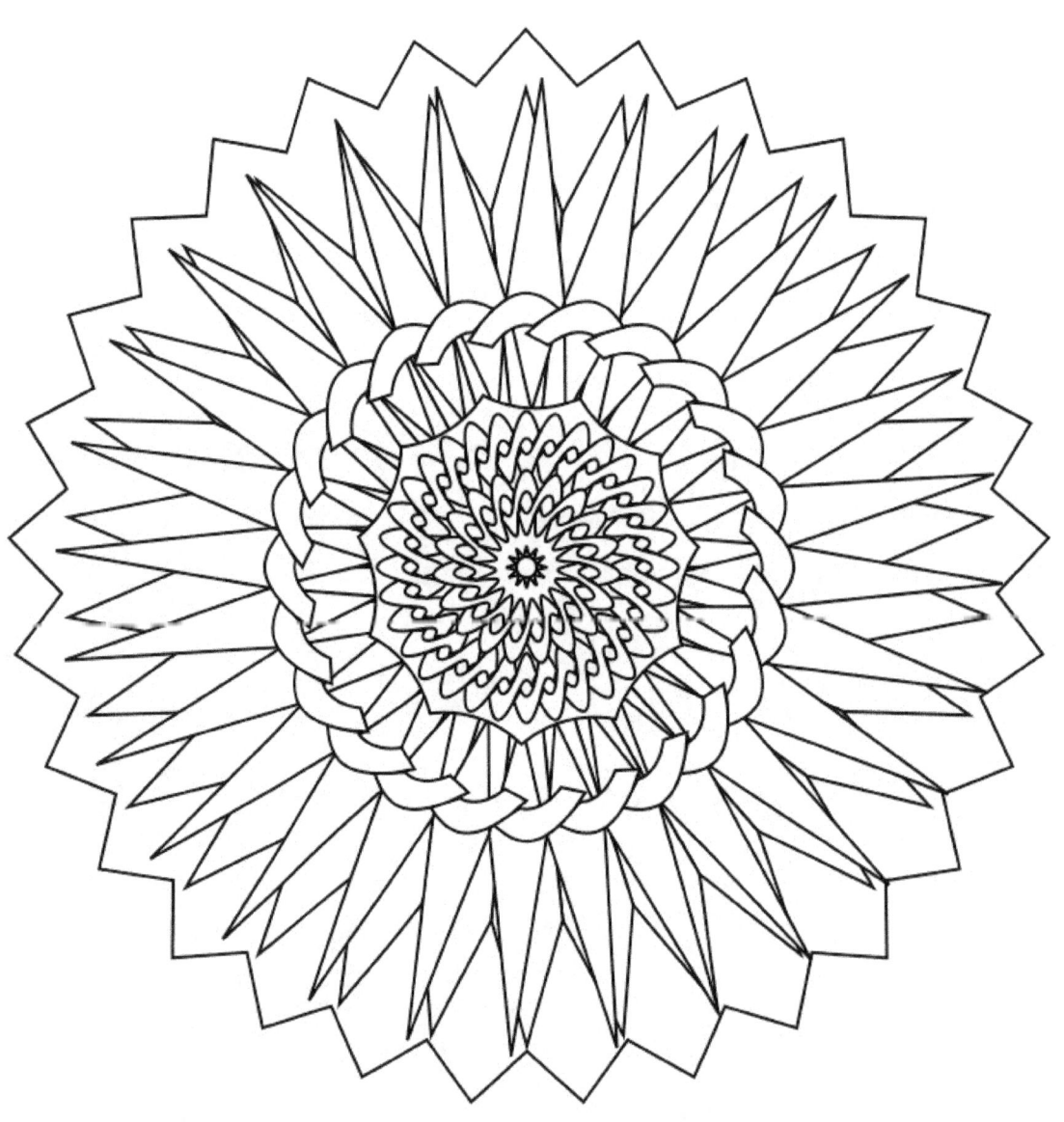

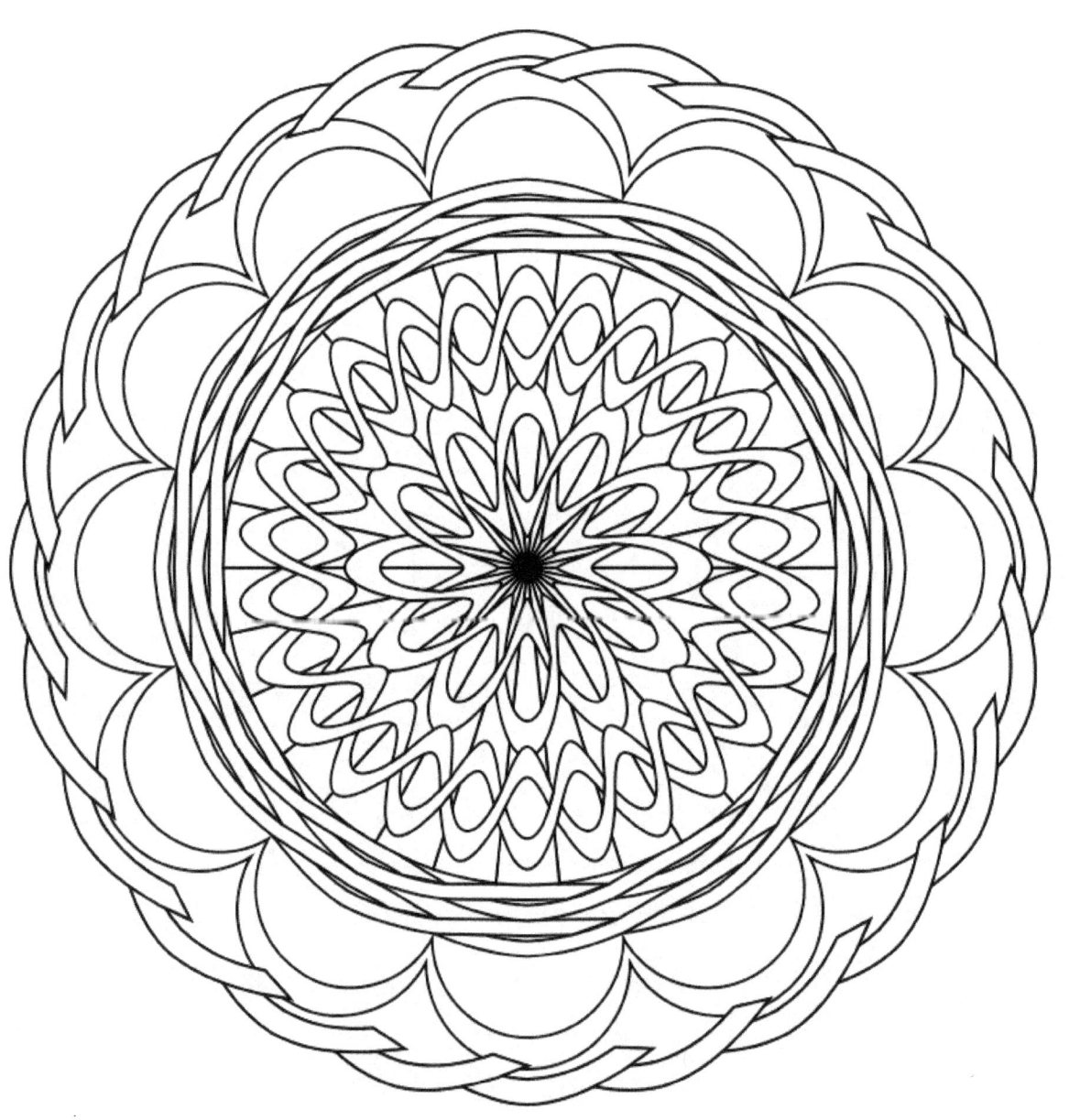

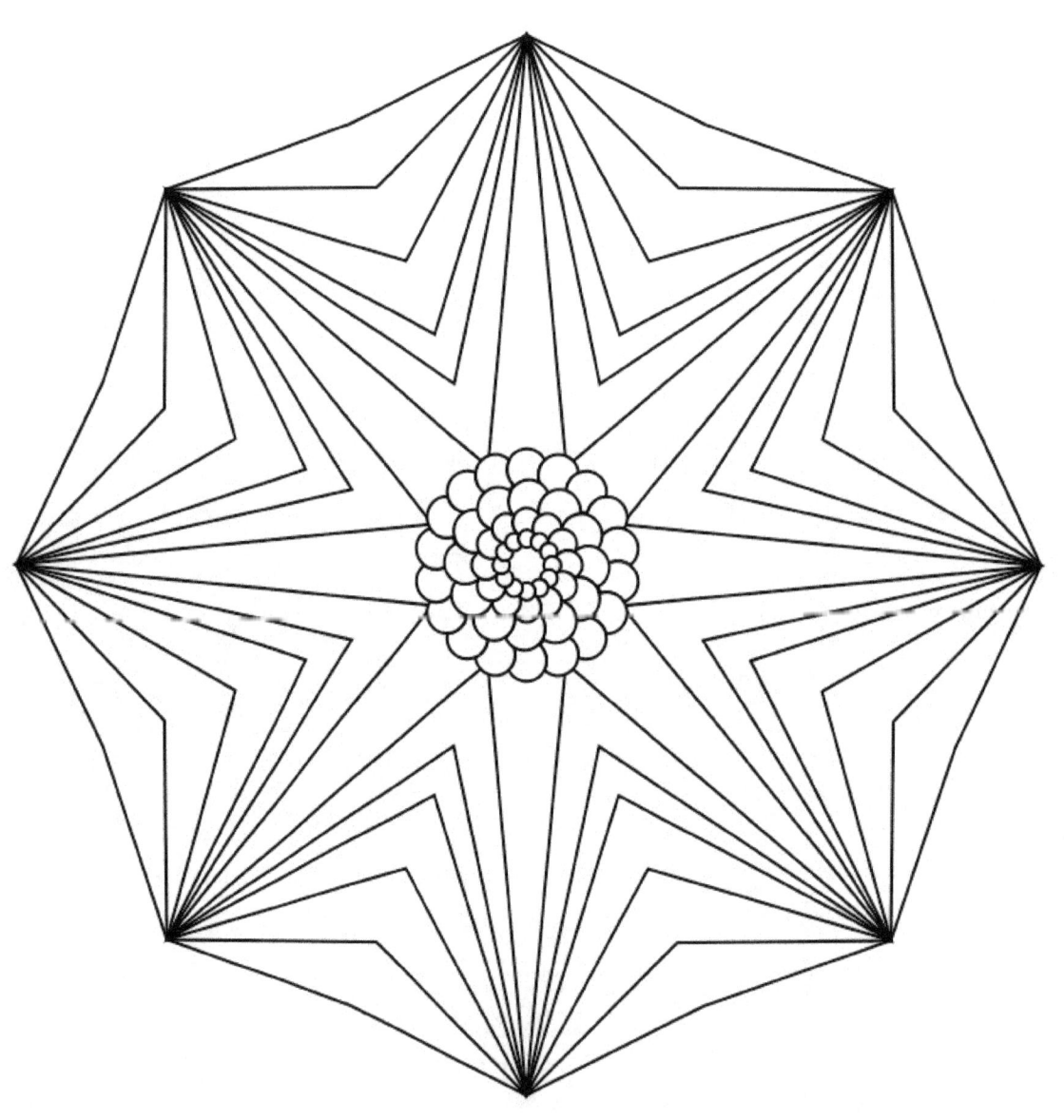

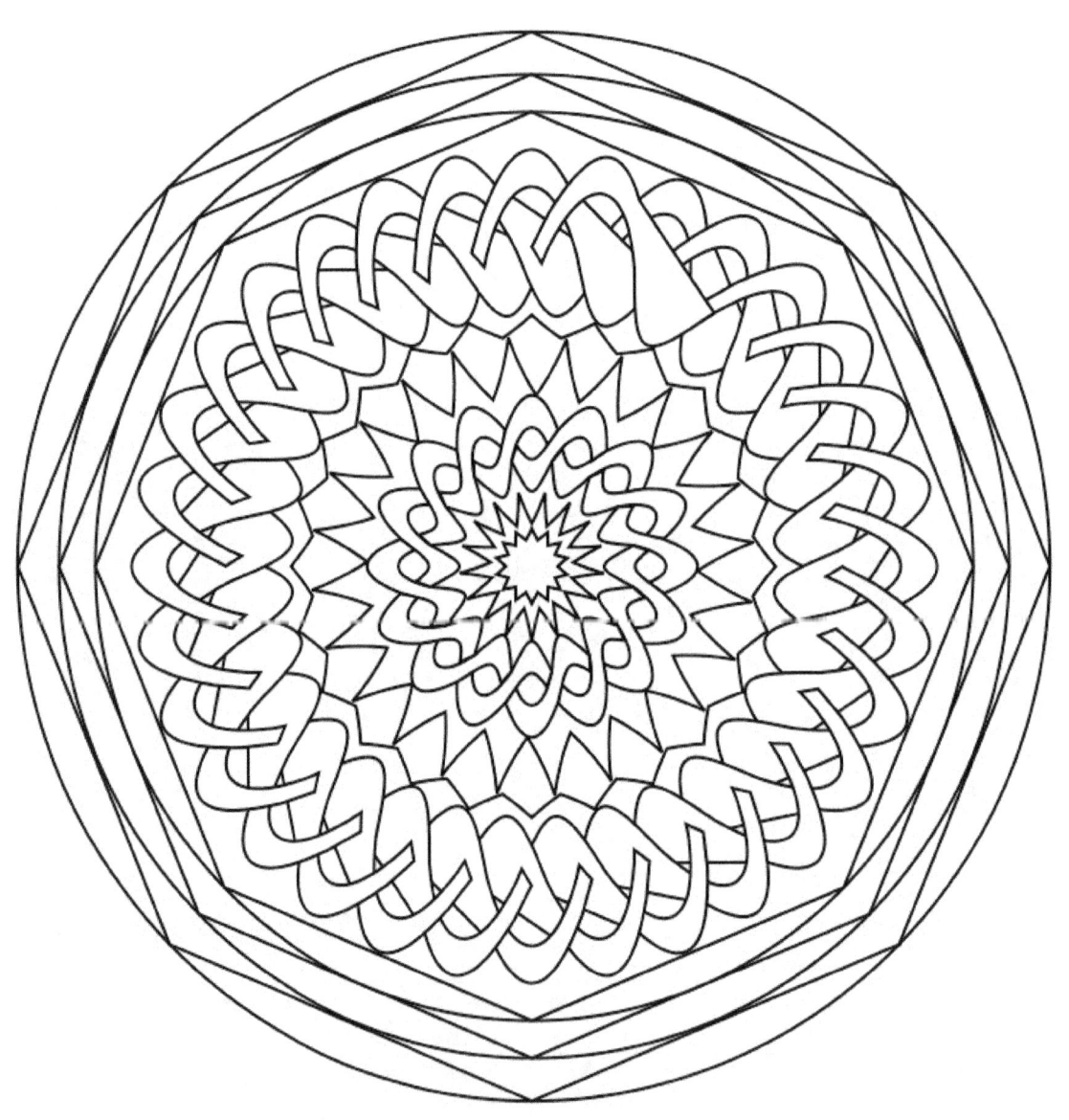

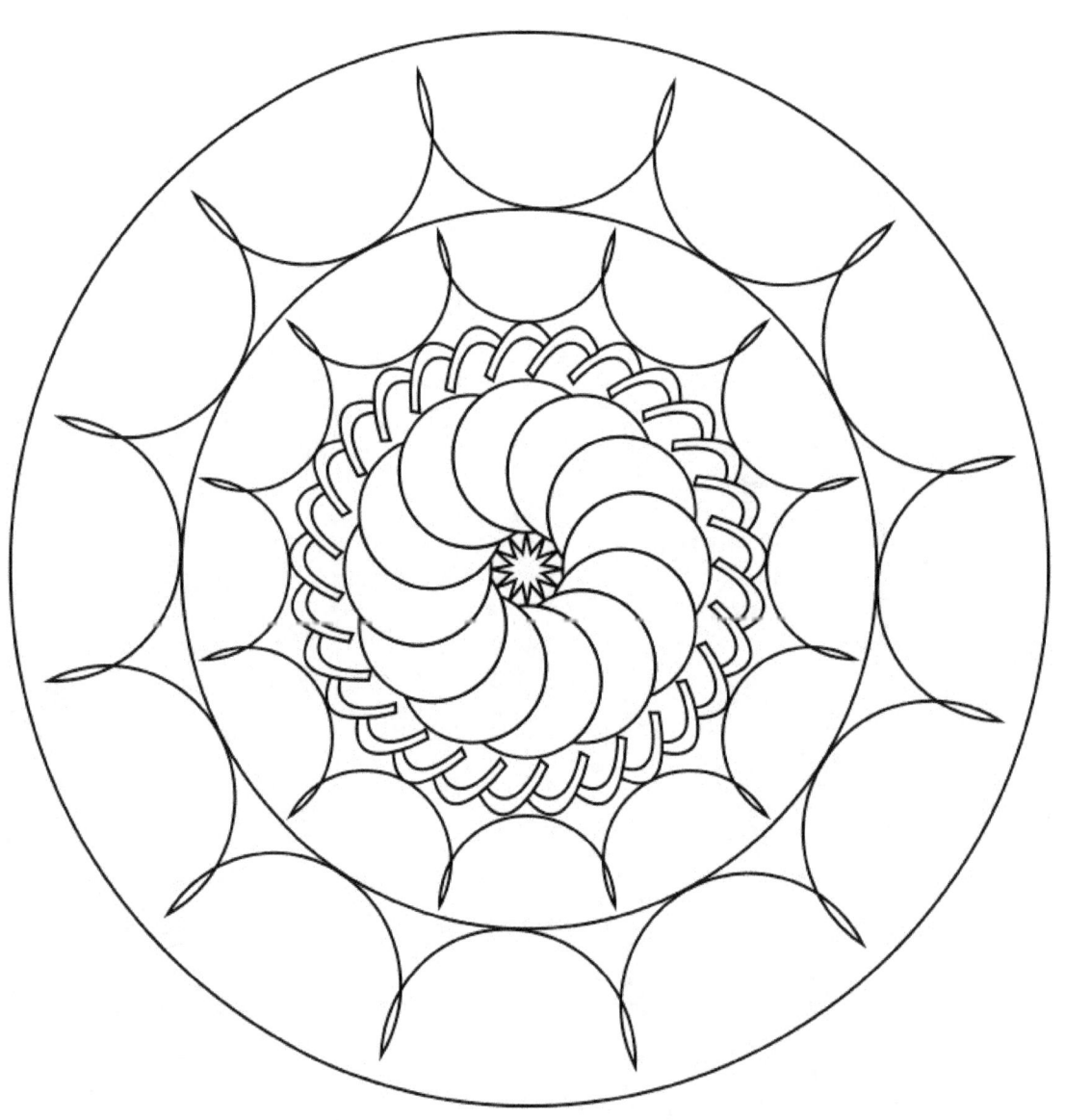

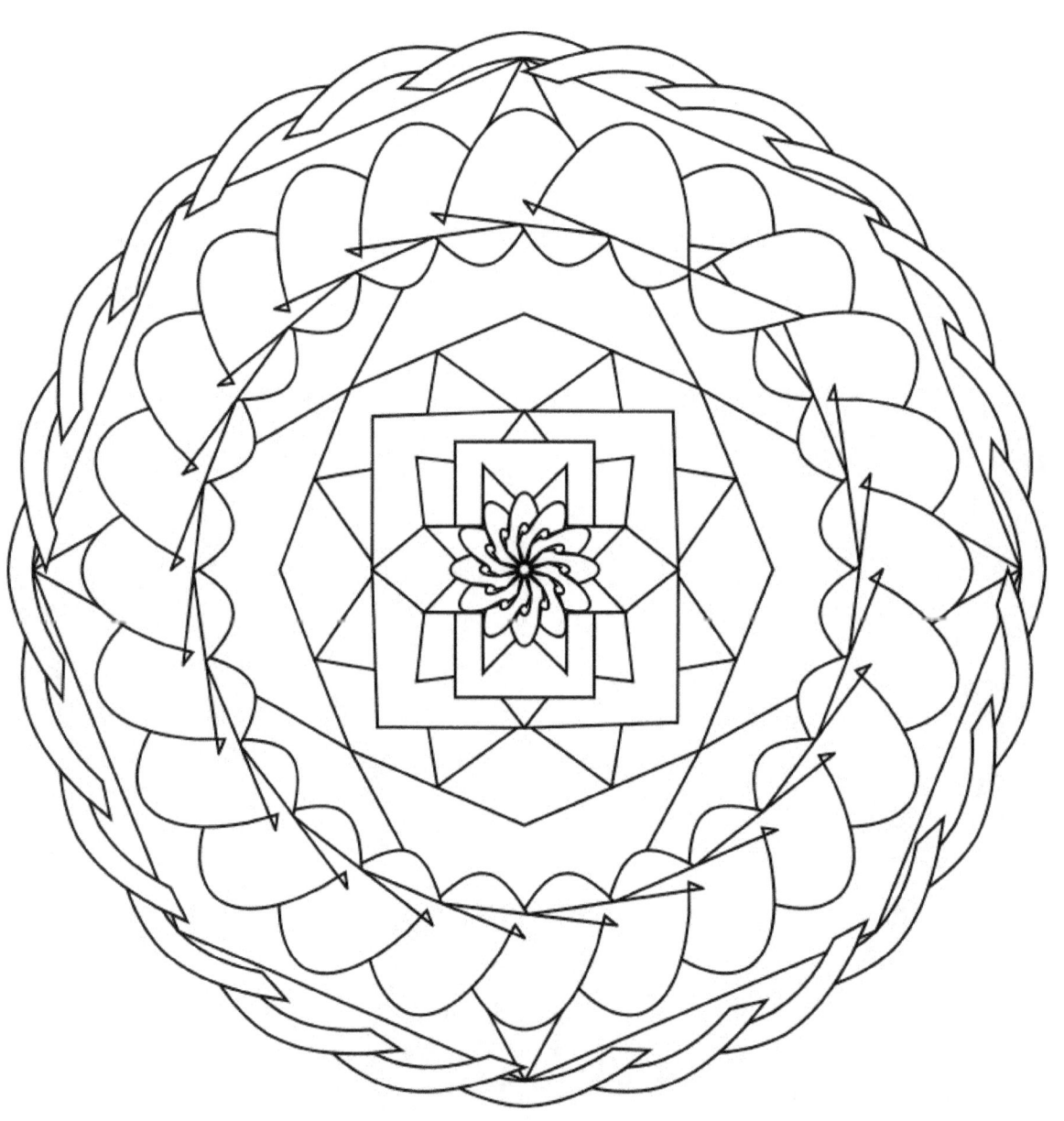

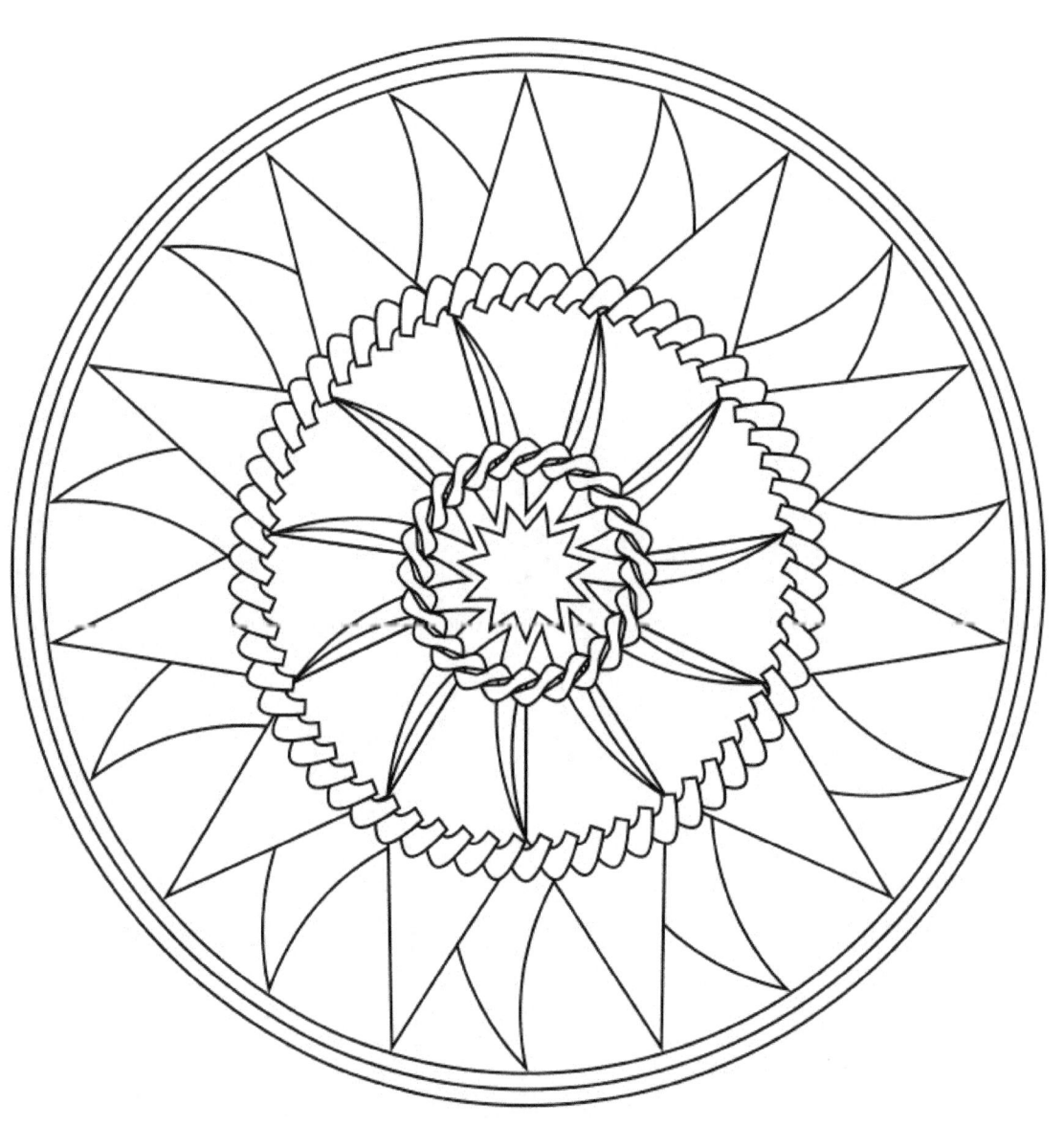

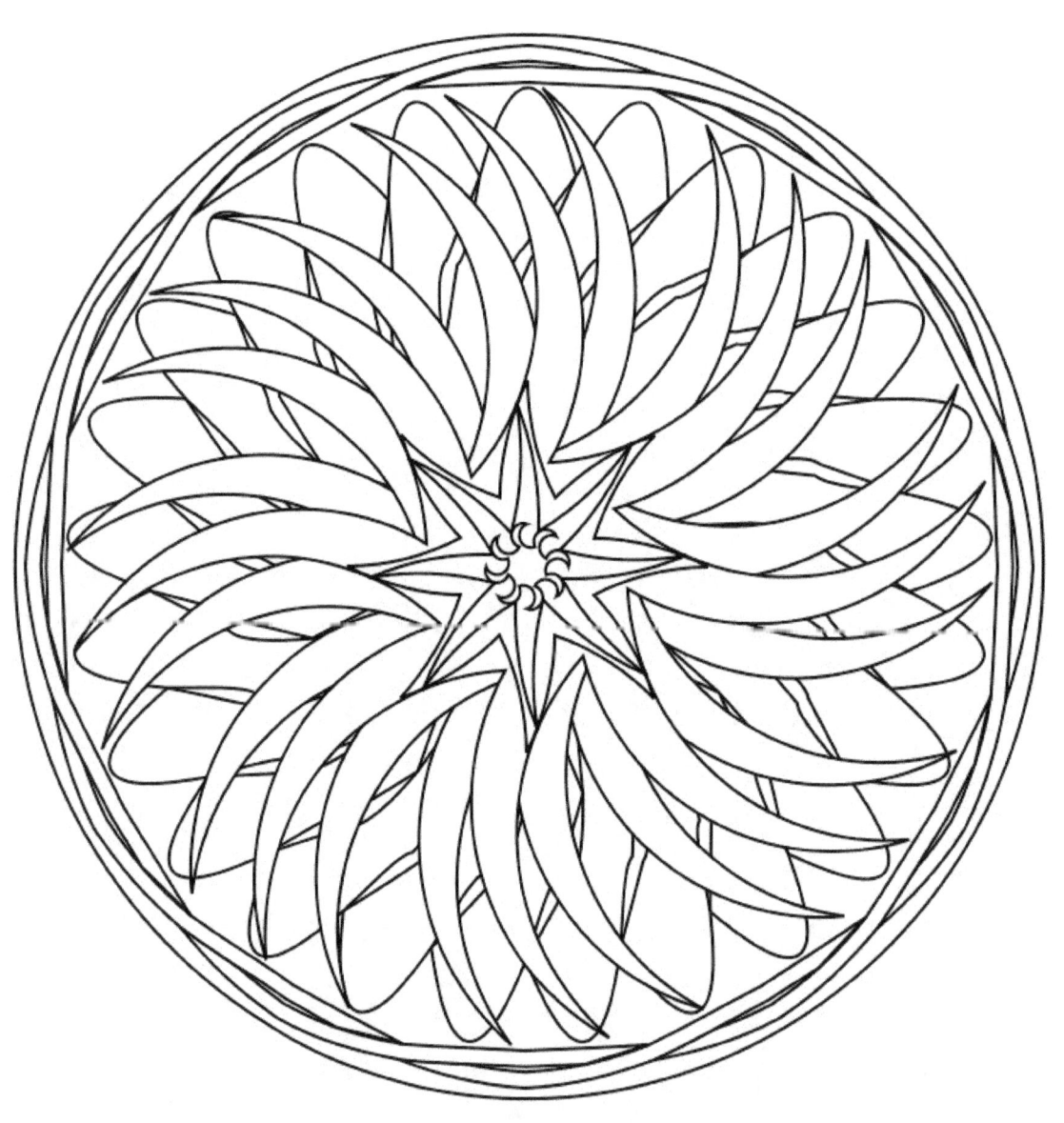

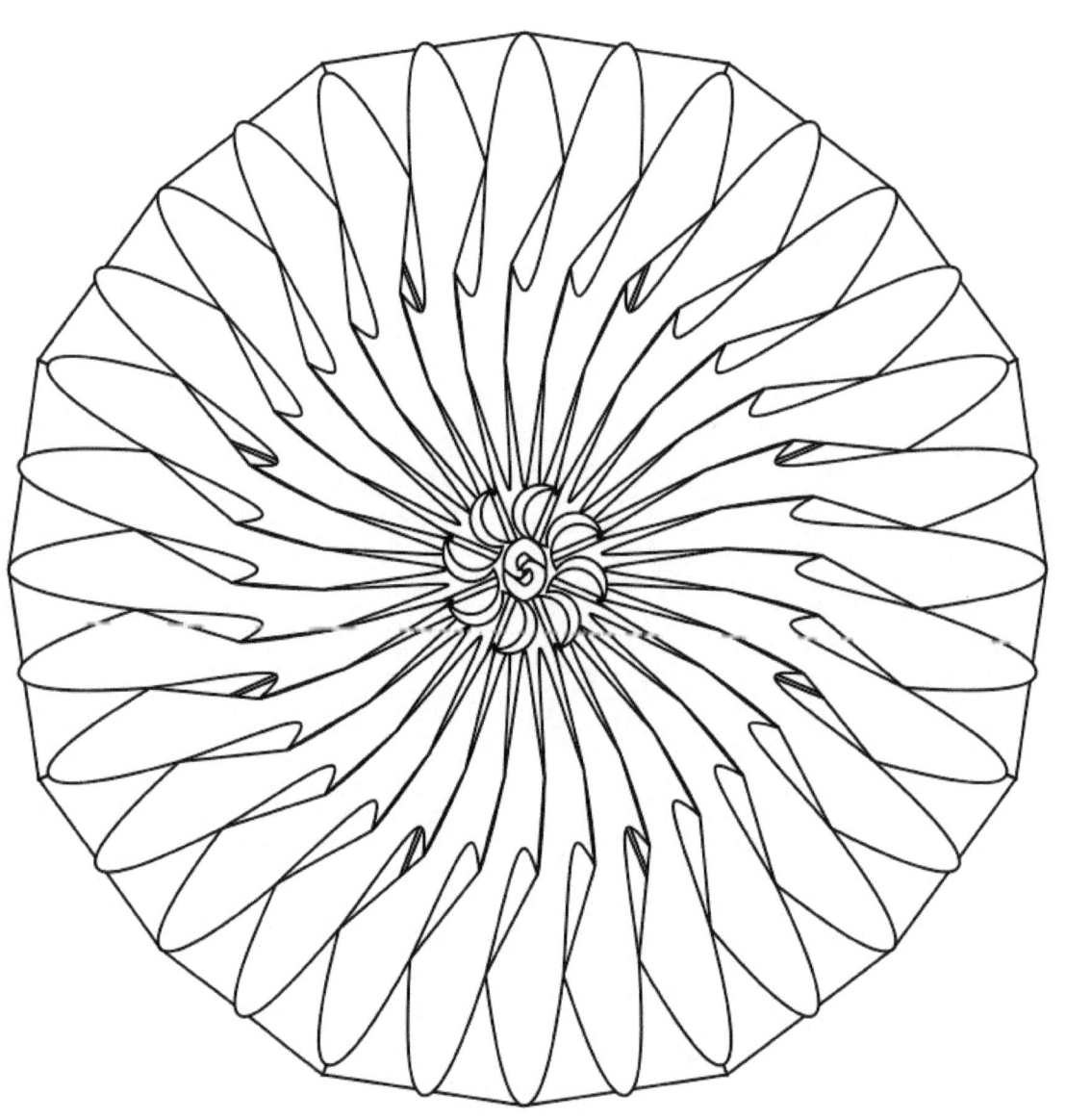

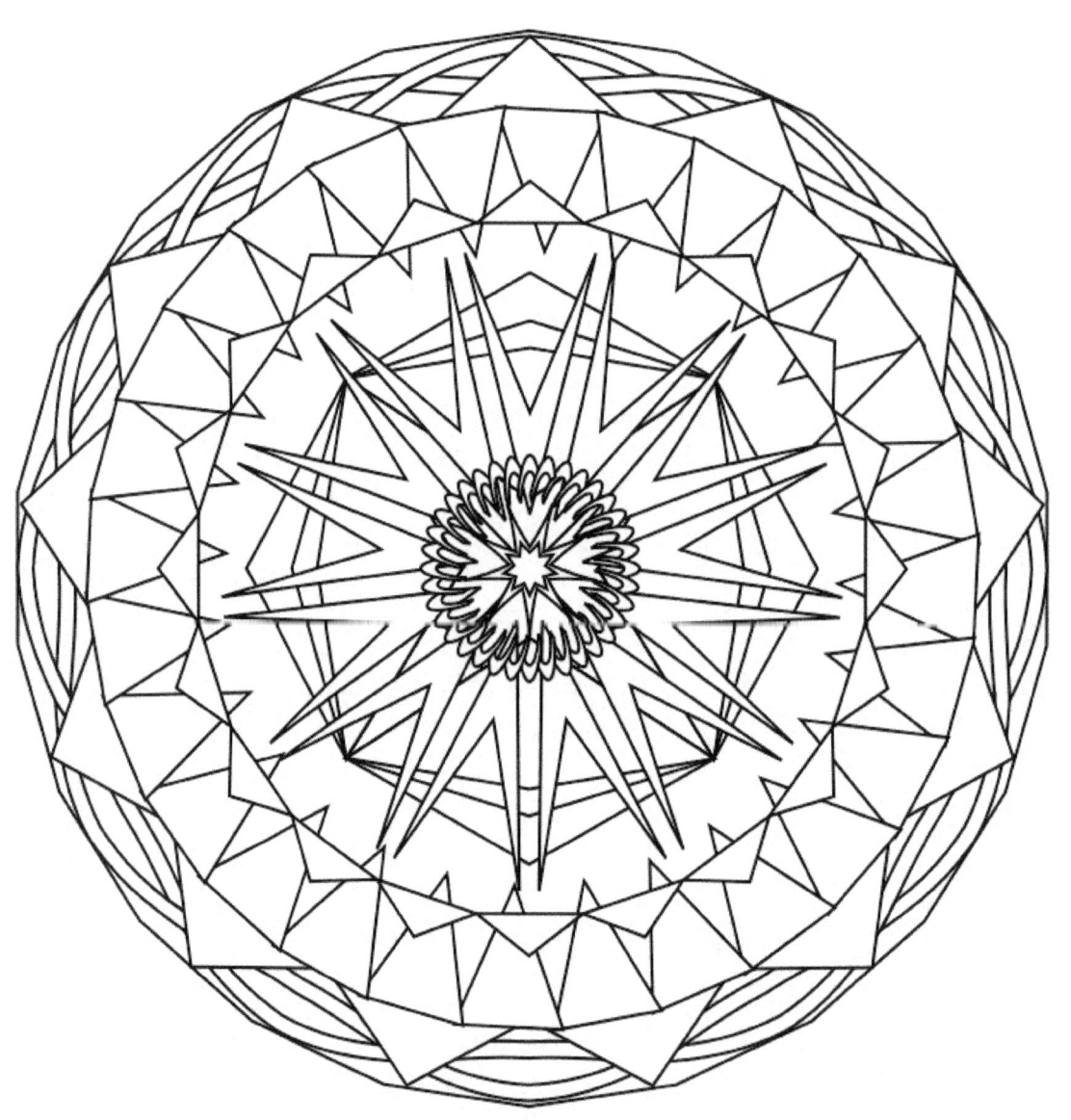

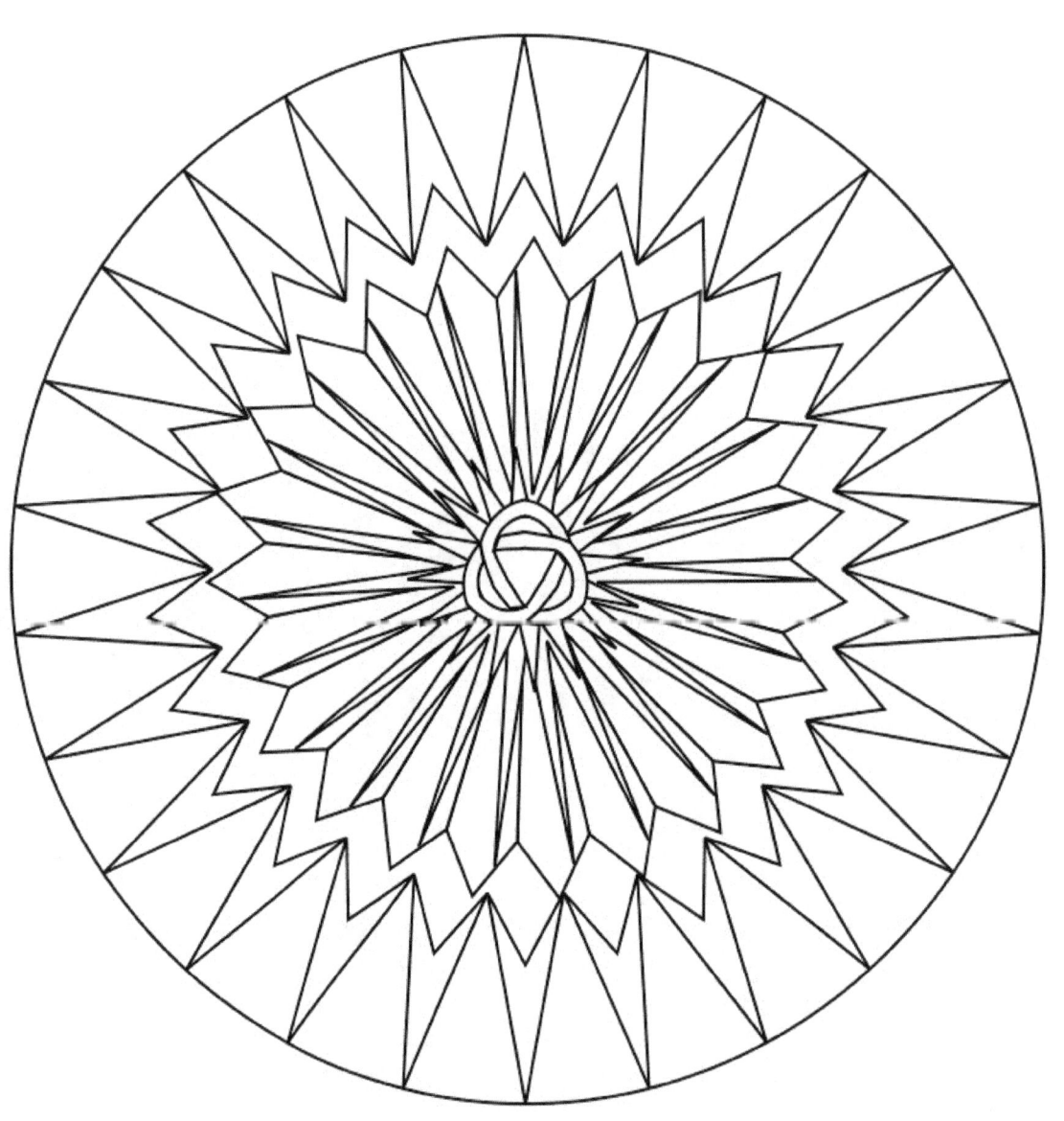

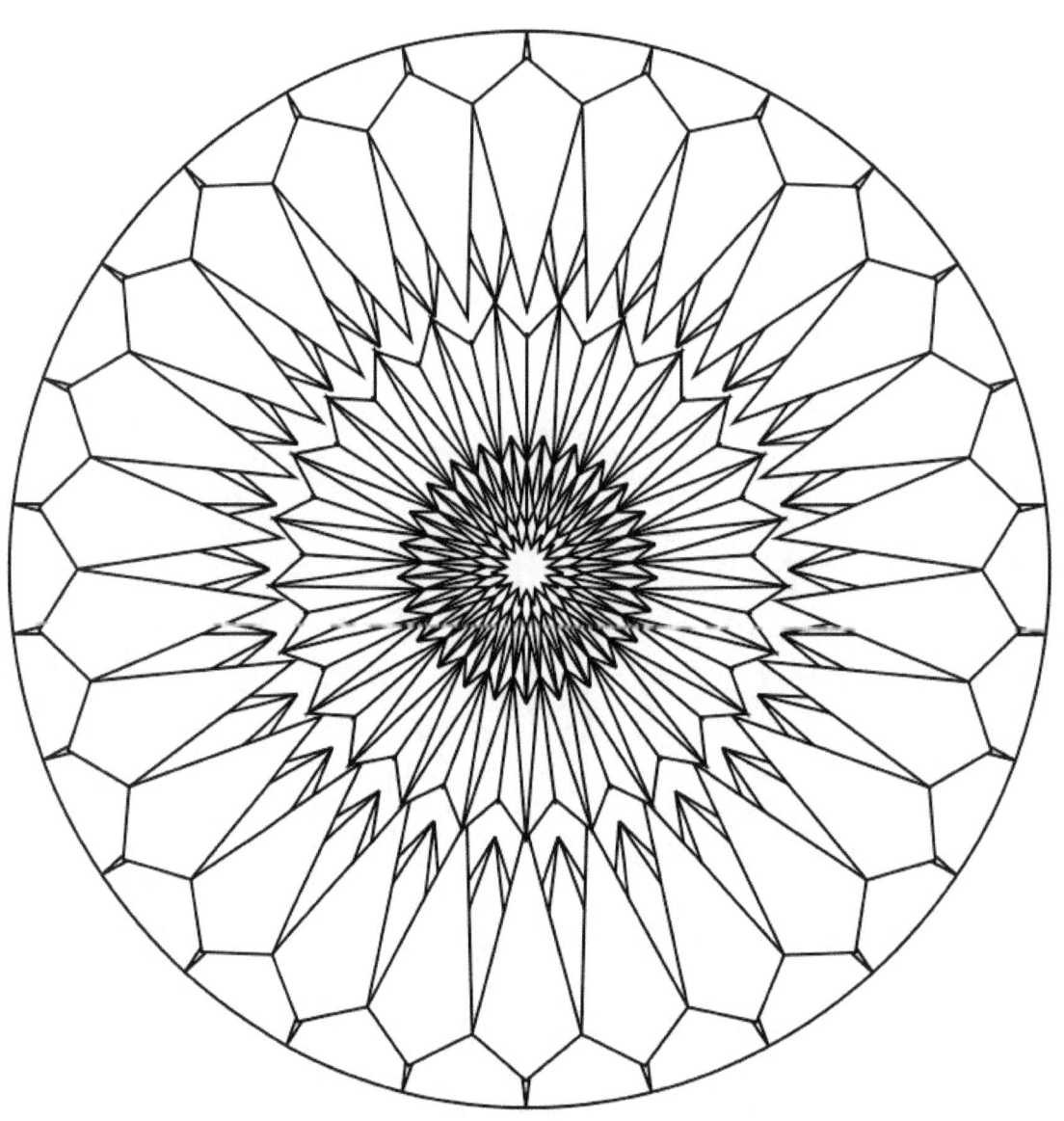

Be sure to look for more coloring books from Lena Kez.

Thank you!

www.ingramcontent.com/pod-product-compliance
Lightning Source LLC
Chambersburg PA
CBHW080610180526
45168CB00007B/2850